The Beginning of Words
Words
How English Grew

Colin Pickles and Laurence Meynell
Designed and illustrated by Don Heywood

G.P. Putnam's Sons · New York

Contents

Introduction

This book is about how the English language grew. Most of its growth took place in England, but right from the earliest days England has been visited by people coming across the sea from all parts of the world. Sometimes they came with armies as invaders; sometimes with goods as traders, sometimes as religious missionaries with new ideas. They all had one thing in common however—they all brought new words to enrich our English language.

In like fashion British sailors and explorers, when they came back from their adventurous journeys in foreign parts, brought with them new and often exciting words to add to our vocabulary. Gradually they established colonies in other continents and these colonies in time became independent nations. In these countries the English language continued to grow and many new, vivid words were added to it, reflecting the experiences and customs of the peoples of these countries. The result is a language spoken more widely than any other in the world and having one of the richest vocabularies.

The story of English from its small beginnings to its present international use is told in the following pages. Hundreds of words and expressions are traced to their sources in the history not just of one island but of a large part of the world. By understanding how these words began one can learn to use them with greater pleasure and skill. And, as the last chapter shows, one can invent new ones. For a language is not a fixed thing. It may have a beginning, but it cannot have an end. It never will stop growing.

Note: Where a word may have more than one accepted spelling, the original English spelling is given first and the alternate spelling follows in brackets.

1 Greek

The Greek civilization may seem very remote to us and the fact that in the Greek alphabet the letters are not written like ours may put you off trying to learn the language, yet strangely enough the names of many of the most modern things which we use every day in this scientific age come from the Greek language.

But first of all, let us look at a word used in the last paragraph, the word **alphabet**. The first two letters in Greek are *alpha*, our 'A', and *beta*, our 'B'; put them together and you have alphabet, just as we say ABC.

Tele- is the Greek word meaning from afar off, or at a distance. *Phone* is the Greek for a voice or a sound; so when Alexander Graham Bell invented an instrument by which sounds and voices could be heard over a great distance it was called a **telephone.**

If *phone* is the Greek for sound, can you think of a meaning for the word **phonetics**? Compare your answer with what the dictionary says.

This Greek word *tele-* meaning at a distance comes in a number of other terms we use today. The **telegraph**, for instance, is something which enables you to write at a distance, and you can probably work out **telegram**, **telephoto** and **television** for yourself.

The word telephoto will make you realize that the Greeks had a word *photos* meaning light, so when the camera was invented the pictures which it took by means of light were called **photographs**, things drawn by means of light.

Another way of using light to send messages was to employ the rays of the sun. The Greek word for sun is *helios* and the device for signalling by means of reflecting its rays is called a **heliograph**.

Nowadays you can hardly pick up a paper without seeing the word **democracy**. This comes to us direct from the two Greek words *demos* meaning the people and *kratos* meaning power. Look up the meaning of the words **autocracy** and **autocrat**.

Quite a number of English terms are connected with the Greek word meaning to measure which is *metron*. There is an altimeter, for instance, which measures how high a plane is flying; then we have a **speedometer** which measures speed and a **pedometer** which tells you how far you have walked. Look up the word biped in the Latin section.

Philo in Greek meant loving or fond of, and you will find it in a number of English words, the **philharmonic** orchestra for instance is one made up of lovers of harmony. Look up **philosopher** and, particularly if you are a stamp collector, **philately** in your dictionary.

An **athlete** is one who contends for a prize because the Greek word for prize was *athlon*, which is very suitable seeing that the Greeks originated the Olympic Games.

A particular kind of athlete is an **acrobat** which originally meant some one who balanced on his toes; it comes from the Greek word *akron* which means a point.

If you get in a **panic** over anything you are seized with the groundless sort

of fear which the Greek god *Pan* was thought to cast like a spell over people.

Cyclon in Greek means a circle or a round thing and so a wheel. A machine with two wheels is a **bicycle**. How many wheels has a **tricycle** and what other words can you think of beginning with *tri-*?

A **micrometer** is an instrument for measuring small distances or units because the Greek word for small is *micros*. So a **microbe** is a small unit of life and a **microscope** is a device for looking at small objects. Compare it with **telescope**. Look at what was said about telephone and try to think what **microphone** means. The word for movement in Greek is *kinema* so the first moving pictures were called the Kinematograph in English which has become softened and shortened into the **cinema**.

2 Roman

Britain was a province of Rome for more than 300 years and the Roman legions did not finally leave until the year 410 A.D.

The Roman word for a **camp** or fortified place was *castrum*. In England there are plenty of towns whose modern names show that they were built by the Romans; there is **Doncaster**, for example, and **Dorchester**, **Winchester** and many more. In the United States there are towns like **Rochester** named after such English towns.

The Roman soldiers had to get from one castrum, or fortified town, to the next easily and quickly. To do this they built a wonderful system of roads. The Roman word for a road was *strata via* which means a paved way, and the first part of this term is now our English word **street**. Two of the great Roman roads in England were Watling Street and Ermine Street. If a Roman road crossed a river, would you expect the place where it did so to be called *'street-ford'?* There is Stratford-on-Avon in England where Shakespeare was born. There are twelve Stratfords in the United States and one in Canada.

Along the splendid roads which the Romans built were placed stones to mark distances. These were put at every thousand paces; the Latin word for a thousand is *mille* so the distance became known as a **mile** and the stones were called **milestones**.

When a man finished his service in the Roman Legions, he was very often given a plot of land in a military settlement which the Romans called a *colonia*; this word was shortened into *coln* and can be seen in such place names as Lin*coln* and *Col*chester. Sometimes people are named after towns. Think of a famous President of the United States.

The Roman word for a harbour (harbor) was portus, from which we get the word **port**. Also names such as Devonport and Portsmouth in England; Bridgeport and Newport in the United States.

A football or baseball **fan** is a person who is a loyal supporter of some particular team, and you may be surprised to know that the word has a religious origin. But it has. Look up the word **fane** in your dictionary and you will find that it comes directly from the Latin word *fanum* meaning a temple. Someone who was constantly in the temple was called a **fanatic**, so anyone who shows excessive enthusiasm for anything is now called a fan.

Quite a number of words connected with religion come to us from the Latin.

The Romans called a **cup** a *calix*; can you think of a modern church word that is derived from this?

Candidus was the Latin word for **white**; a person who was applying for government office in Rome had to wear a white toga. He was called *candidatus* and a **candidate** is what we call people today who are applying for election to local government bodies or Congress or Parliament.

The Roman day was reckoned to start at what we call six o'clock, and they estimated that after nine hours the day was half way through: *nona hora* is the Latin for ninth hour, and nona hora got shortened to **noon** which we still use to describe our midday. The word **afternoon** is in everyday use and **forenoon** is still used occasionally.

By the way, you probably know that **a.m.** means morning and **p.m.** afternoon. A.m. stands for **antemeridian**, and p.m. **post-meridian**. **Ante** is the Roman word for before and **post** for

after. **Meridian** itself means the middle of the day, **medius** meaning middle and **dies** meaning day. What other English words come from the Latin word **medius**? What does **mediocre** mean? What is a **medium**?

The Latin for something placed firmly in a particular position was *positus*, and so we get our word **post**, for example a doorpost or a gatepost. Along the great Roman roads horses were stationed at fixed intervals so that riders could use them in relays. They became known as post-horses. When letters were carried by this means we find the use of the word extended until now we talk about a postage stamp, a postman, and so on.

When we write down words we use a **pen** and until quite recently pens were made from quills or feathers. The Latin for a feather was *penna* which is what our word comes from; and incidentally a **penknife** is so called because it was originally used for sharpening a quill and making a writing instrument out of it. It may interest you to know that a female swan is also called a pen; but this doesn't come from the Latin, and in fact nobody knows where it does come from. Do you know what a male swan is called?

If you share your food with somebody he is your **companion** which comes from two Latin words *cum* meaning with and *panis* meaning bread.

This Latin preposition *cum* (=with) can be seen in many English words, for instance **compassion** which means a feeling with somebody. Sometimes it gets changed to *col* as in **collision**, or to *con* as in **contend**.

A number of Latin prepositions are used like this in English. The Latin word meaning **against**, for instance, is *contra*. To speak against a person is to **contradict** him, *contra* meaning against and *dicere* meaning to speak. Can you think of three other English words starting with contra- or contro-?

In the same way *bis* in Latin meant two or twice. A **biscuit** is a thing *bis coctus* or twice cooked. A **biped** is an animal with two feet, a **bicycle** has two wheels. What does **bilateral** mean?

When a British housewife goes shopping she will probably call at the fishmonger or the ironmonger. The last part of all these words, **-monger**, comes from the Latin word *mango* which simply meant a trader.

If a person goes out of his mind and begins to rave we say he is **delirious**. This is a very interesting word because it goes right back to what is really at the base of everything, agriculture and the earth. The Latin for a furrow made by the plough was *dira*; if you started to go away from normal, right lines you went out of—*de* is the Latin for out of or from—the proper furrow lines— hence delirious.

In the last paragraph the word **agriculture** was used. Incidentally it comes from the Latin word for a field which is *ager*; the old god of agriculture was *Saturn* and his name is given to one of the days of our week, Saturn's day. Can you find out what the names of the other days come from?

Instead of looking into a crystal ball to read fortunes, as some people do today, the Roman fortune tellers studied the flight of birds. The Latin for birds is *aves*, and so we have **aviary**, a place to keep birds. To look in Latin was *specere*. Aves-specere has got corrupted into **auspice** which is now our English word for something which indicates the future.

When you eat your **cereal** for breakfast spare a thought for the Roman goddess of corn and flowers who was called Ceres after whom your cereal is named.

3

The Greek and Roman influences on our language have been discussed first because those languages are much older than ours. The basic stock of our language is really Anglo-Saxon, which was brought to England by invading tribes from the Continent during the fifth and sixth centuries A.D. It was the Angles who gave the name to our language—English—though it was the

Saxons who came first, but the languages of these two tribes were so alike that we can call them both Saxon.

These tribes took over surprisingly few words from the country dwelling Britons, speaking a language known as Celtic, whom they drove into the western and northern parts of the British Isles—Cornwall, Wales, Scotland and Ireland. Welsh, Gaelic and Irish are all Celtic in origin. The word **Sassenach**, still used by the Welsh and the Scots to describe the English, is the Celtic word for the Saxons.

Latin influenced our language, as described in the last chapter, partly because the invading tribes borrowed many words from the Romanized town dwellers they found living in England and partly because the Roman missionaries converted England to Christianity during the sixth and seventh centuries. Much later many more Latin and also Greek words entered our language as it became necessary to describe the more complicated things and ideas our developing civilization required. We borrowed such words from these 'classical' languages, Greek and Latin, because they were spoken by educated people all over Europe and had an international reputation.

For these reasons ordinary things of daily use and experience are often of Saxon origin, while more complicated ideas like democracy or altitude come from Greek or Latin. Such words as **day**, **night**, **dew**, **darkness**, **light** and **dawn** are all Saxon.

Next time you are in a field take a look at a **daisy**. It has a yellow centre (center) surrounded by white petals like rays of light; it looks like a miniature sun, and since the sun is the eye of the day the Saxons called this humble little flower the *daeges eage*, that is day's eye or as we now say daisy.

When you were in the field looking at the daisy you might give a thought to the word **field** itself which is also a Saxon word. For a long time a great deal of England was covered with forest and scrub-like growth. As the population increased more land was continually needed for cultivation so there was a constant urge to clear away the forests. This was done by felling the trees and an area so cleared was said to be *feld*.

In those Saxon fields the **herdsman**, *herd* as in **goatherd** and **shepherd**, looked after their **oxen**, **sheep**, **calves** and **swine**. Now turn to the section about Norman French words and see what is said about **beef**, **mutton**, **veal** and **pork**.

You can now realize that while the animals were alive they were looked after by the Saxon farmworkers, but when they were killed and ready for the table it was the Norman overlords who had the pleasure of eating them.

Both **sun** and **moon** come direct from Saxon words: *sunne* meaning that which produces anything, because the sun was regarded as the source of all heat and life and *mona* the measurer of time because the **months** were fixed by it. The first days of our week, **Sunday** and **Monday**, are still called after the sun and moon. One particular Sunday in the year is called **Whitsunday**, which we generally shorten to *Whit*sun, meaning white, because in old times penitents wore white robes at church services on the feast of Pentecost which is when Whitsunday occurs.

The moon was mentioned in the last paragraph and there are two Saxon words used in connection with it: when it is getting larger in the heavens we say it is **waxing**, and when it is getting smaller we say it is **waning**. Incidentally the old farmers will tell you that it is always best to sow any seeds when the moon is waxing and not when it is waning.

If somebody is short tempered and rude you sometimes call him **churlish**, this is a Saxon word coming directly from *churl*. In feudal times there were three ranks of freemen: an earl, a thane and a churl. The churls therefore were the lowest class of freemen; they frequently lacked manners and this lack of manners was called churlishness.

A few minutes study of a map will tell you a good deal about Saxon names. You will certainly find a number of places the names of which end in *-ton*. England is full of them: Skipton, Warrington, Preston, Bilston, to take four quick examples. *Ton* is the Saxon word for a place surrounded by a hedge or palisade, hence a fortified place, and finally a **town**; *ham*, think of Oakham, Petersham, Caterham, and so on, means much the same but it indicates more of a dwelling place, a **home** which is the same word, than somewhere fortified.

Burn was the Saxon word for a stream and you can see two examples of it today in London, Holborn and Tyburn, which commemorate districts where not very long ago open streams, now piped underground, used to run.

Ley was what the Saxons called an open space in the middle of woodlands and a map will show you plenty of examples. Henley is one. In contrast to this *hurst* meant an area of dense woodland and there are plenty of these too, Lyndhurst and Midhurst for example.

The Saxon word meaning to bend was *bugan* and from the first syllable of this we eventually got the word **bow**, the bent thing which, with its missile the arrow, was the Saxons' main hunting weapon.

If you say that a certain thing was very **cheap** you mean that it was inexpensive to buy; and the Saxon word *ceap* meant just that—to buy. In time the word also came to mean the place where you could buy things, or the market, as, for instance, Cheapside in London, and a town which held a large or celebrated market sometimes showed the fact in its name, Chipping Norton, for example, in the Cotswold hills in England, means Norton where a *ceaping* or market was held.

You may occasionally come across the word **cheapjack** which merely means a hawker, a man who comes round with a tray or box of small goods for sale, someone who brings the market-place to your door.

4

Some time after the Anglo-Saxon invasions, the Danes and other Scandinavians began to sail across the North Sea in their famous long ships. They first appeared in 787 and between 866 and 875 made constant raids and indeed won and held a great deal of English land. You can see a picture of a Viking raid on page 15. Notice their horned helmets. Alfred the Great was the man who ultimately defeated them in 897 and if you want to read a fine poem about Alfred and the Danes read G. K. Chesterton's 'Ballad of the White Horse'. The White Horse was the banner under which Alfred's men fought. But in 1015 the Danes were back again; their King Canute landed in England in that year and one year later (1016) was acknowledged King of England so that from 1016 to 1042 England was actually ruled by a Danish King. The Danes left many marks on our language.

-by
The Danish word for a settlement or small town was *byr*. When this was tacked on to other words, especially in England, the final r got lost, so in the eastern counties which were the principal parts occupied by the Danes, you will still find plenty of towns ending in -*by*; e.g. Hunmanby, Whitby, Carnaby, Wetherby. All these are in Yorkshire; get out an atlas and see how many you can find in Lincolnshire where the Danes first settled in England.

Husband
Originally this meant a man who dwelt in a house, the Danish words were *hus* = house and *bondi* = a person who lived there. A peasant who lived in a house was almost inevitably married so it came to mean the man who had a wife and was master of the household.

Law
The Danish word for it was *lagu* which meant something which was laid down. A by-law is a law relating to a particular town. See what was said about -by above. An out-law was a man who by some act had put himself outside the protection of the law.

Snub, snare
The Danish words were almost identical with our present ones—*snubba* and *snara*; the Danes were fond of words beginning with *sn-*; you may be able to find some more in your dictionary.

Awkward
Awk which came to us from the Danes means turned the wrong way and the *ward* part is added for emphasis just as in backward or forward.

Riding
There is a word 'riding' peculiar to England, which really means a 'third-ing'. Yorkshire, where the Danes settled in great force, is divided into three: east, west and north. This word has nothing to do with riding horseback.

Brink
The edge of some steep place—*brinka* in Danish.

Sky
This is a Danish word; with them it originally meant the clouds.

Window
The *vindauga* or wind eye because the first use of a window was to let in the wind and the smoke out—long before fireplaces and chimneys were thought of.

Score
Skor was the word the Danes used for cutting a notch on anything and we still used the word in the same sense. The scores at the game of cricket used to be recorded by cutting a notch on a piece of wood for each run.

Crook
Krokr was their word for it, meaning something which was curled over or bent like a shepherd's crook. A man whose character is bent away from what it ought to be is called a crook in modern slang.

Skill
The Danes had a verb *skilja* meaning to divide or distinguish between things closely alike. If you could do this you were thought to be clever so skill came to be equated with cleverness.

Scales

A *skal* was a bowl, and the two bowls used for weighing purposes became called the scales.

Thrift

From the verb *thrifa* meaning to grasp. If you were grasping you thrived and so had thrift. It is also the name of a wildflower. Can you think why?

Reindeer

The deer which were used for transport and so had to be trained and controlled by a *rein*. Take a look at the page about Latin words to see the difference between this sort of rein and the reign of a king.

5 Norman

The Normans, led by William I, invaded and conquered England in 1066 at the Battle of Hastings. They were fine builders of stone churches and castles and enthusiastic hunters; they set great store on orderly government and on the importance of law. Many of the words which we have inherited from them are concerned with these activities. If you are learning French you may be able to find out by yourself how many of such words came to us.

Curfew
As an aid to preventing fire and maintaining order the Normans insisted on people being within doors with fires extinguished, at a certain time each evening. *Couvre-feu* means cover the fire.

Parlour (parlor)
Originally the room in a monastery where it was permissible to speak. The Norman word for to speak was *parler*.

Parliament
Do you think this word has any connection with the last?

Mortgage
A pledge, or gage, on something which is dead, *mort*; when you get a mortgage on your house you give a pledge for the repayment of the money you borrow based on the property itself, a dead thing.

Warrant
Before a police officer can search your house for any reason he has to have a warrant to do so—the Old French word was *warand* and it is connected with guarantee; *gu* and *w* frequently get mixed up in derivations.

Chancellor
In Norman times in England, as now one of the great officers of state; originally he was a sort of usher who when on duty stood at the bar of the law court. *Cancelli* was the Latin word for bars or barriers, which gave the Norman word *chancelier*.

Master
There are all sorts of masters: a master of arts (M.A.); the captain, or master, of a ship; a schoolmaster; there is also a magistrate, a rather superior sort of master in the legal sense. **Master** became **mister**, which has been shortened to **Mr.** as a title to go before a man's name.

Reward
The Norman word was *reguard*. (Remember what was said about *gu* and *w*.) If you had proper regard for a person's worth and the work he had done you probably felt inclined to reward him for it.

Sovereign
The Norman feudal system laid great stress on sovereignty—their word was *soverain* which merely meant one who was above somebody else. It wasn't until 1500 that the word was used for the English gold coin and now that paper money has come in that use of the word has almost disappeared.

Count
Originally the area of land owned, or looked after by a Count, the Norman word was *conte*. In the English nobility there isn't a Count but oddly enough

there is a Countess who is the wife of an Earl.

Castle
The Normans built many castles in England a number of which, some in ruins, can be seen today, e.g., Lewes and Arundel. These castles had moats around them for protection, and high battlements. A drawbridge across the moat allowed access.

Beef, mutton, veal, pork
These are all Norman words to describe things we eat. If you look on the page dealing with Saxon words you will see that the Saxons had different names for the same things. Why was this?

Dandelion
Look at a dandelion the next time you are in a field and see if you think its leaves are shaped like the teeth of a lion. The Normans called it *dent-de-lion*.

---

6 Dutch

The Dutch have had three distinct influences on our language.

First in the time of Edward III (1327–77) several waves of Dutch weavers came to England. They settled naturally enough in the nearest part which is now called East Anglia.

Then for more than two hundred years during the seventeenth and eighteenth centuries the English and the Dutch were often at war with each other, particularly at sea. This resulted in the English adopting a number of Dutch sea words.

Thirdly, as a result of the Boer War in South Africa (1899–1902), a number of Dutch words were brought into our language.

Botch is one of the Dutch weavers' words which we have taken over. It means to do a piece of work clumsily, a 'botched-up job' is one badly and untidily done. Sometimes the word gets slightly distorted into **bodge**, and in the wood trade in parts of England a rough and ready worker is still called a **bodger**

Scoff, the slang word meaning to

eat, comes to us from the Dutch.

A **boor** is the term we now use to mean a person without any manners; originally the Dutch word *boer* simply meant a farmer or peasant. In East Anglia to this day one farmer passing another towards evening time will say 'good night bor'. The word 'nigh' means close to, as you probably know, so what do you think neighbour (neighbor) really means?

Waggon, or wagon, you can spell it with one 'g' or two, comes from the Dutch *wagen*. The old English word **wain**, meaning a large farm cart, comes from the same root, and in the West Country when a farmer wants to talk about what in other parts is called the waggon-shed he calls it a wain house.

The Dutch have an expressive word *rabbelen* which means to speak in a quick and confused way, so a whole crowd of people speaking and shouting together became known as a **rabble** which is our word for the same thing today.

There are at least two words connected with painting which have come to us from the Dutch. The Dutch word for an ass is *ezel*, and just as we speak of a clothes-horse, for instance, so they called the wooden frame used by an artist to support his canvas an ass, or ezel, which gives us our word **easel**.

The second artists' term coming from the Dutch is **landscape** for which the Dutch word was *landschap*; the land part is straightforward enough and the ending schap means to shape or make.

When the Dutch sailor wanted to tell a companion to stop doing something, hauling on a rope for instance, he called out *houd vast* which simply meant hold fast. Our sailors took over the phrase and slightly mispronounced it so that in time it became our **avast**. When we come to sea words we cannot do better than to start with **sloop**, from

the Dutch *sloep* which originally meant a small one-masted vessel and then later a small ship of war carrying guns on the upper deck only.

A word often used in connection with ships and shipping is **boom**, one meaning of which is a long wooden spar; this comes to us from the Dutch and is connected with the word **beam**, as, for instance, a wooden beam.

By the way, when you say, for instance, 'there is a great boom in the sale of pictures' you are using an entirely different word. Boom used in this sense belongs to an amusing group of words which are called by the awkward looking name onomatopoeic; this Greek word, which we have adopted into English, means a word which imitates the noise made by the thing you want to describe. So when a child says bow-wow, meaning a dog, or when you talk of the buzzing of bees, the words belong to this onomatopoeic group.

In the same way, boom, in its second sense, simply describes the loud report made by a gun going off; so if any venture or undertaking gets off to a really sensational start it is said to be booming.

Yet another sort of vessel the name of which comes from the Dutch is a **hoy**, the Dutch word for it is *heu* which means a small vessel used for short coastal voyages.

Luff is a yachtsman's term taken directly from the Dutch *loeven* meaning to bring the head of a vessel nearer to the wind. *A-loeven* meant the opposite of this, so our word **aloof** has come to mean keeping away from something, as for instance in the phrase 'he kept aloof from all party politics'.

A very different sort of vessel is a **yacht**, the Dutch name for which was *jaghte*; this word came from the verb *jagen* meaning to hunt, and originally

a yacht was a fast sailing ship largely used by pirates. Yet another type of boat is a **cruiser**; the Dutch word meaning to go backwards and forwards over a thing, to *cross* it, was *kruisen*, and the ships they employed to go backwards and forwards over the oceans guarding their trading fleet they called kruisers from which our word comes.

Why do we call our big passenger carrying boats liners?

7 French

We have seen already on page 16 what a strong influence Norman French had on our English language. This was the natural result of the Norman conquest of England in 1066. By the time Chaucer was writing the Canterbury Tales, about 1370 A.D., the immediate effect of the Normans had worn off. However the kings of England still had large possessions in France and the language spoken at the English court was French. So for some time we went on borrowing many new words from Paris and central France.

The French word for **red** is *rouge*, which we have taken over to describe the powder applied to ladies' cheeks. In the English College of Heralds one of the officials has the splendid title of Rouge Dragon because of the red of his badge.

Our two English words **chivalry** and

cavalry both come directly from the French *cheval* meaning a horse.

When you read about the Cabinet of the President of the U.S.A. or a Prime Minister you can remember that the French word for a room is *cabine*; **cabinet** is a diminutive of this and so means a small room, one used for private talks. So in time the body of politicians who used such a room became known as the Cabinet. We also speak of a **cabin** on board ship, and a **cabinet** is a piece of furniture with small drawers in it

Several words connected with hunting and similar sports come to us from the French. Our word **cover** for example is taken directly from the French *couvrir*. A small copse of trees especially planted to shelter game is called a **covert**, often a fox covert.

Falcon was taken from the French word *faucon*. It is interesting to note that in falconry, which is the sport of flying falcons at smaller birds to kill them, it is only the female bird which is called falcon, the male is called a tiercel.

Rabbit comes to us from old French, the older word for the same little animal was *cony*, which is still used in the fur trade.

The French word for running or riding after anything is *chasser* from which we get our own word **chase** which was originally applied only to going after game, or hunting. A place reserved for hunting was sometimes called a chase and you can still come across this use of the word occasionally as, for example, Cannock Chase in Staffordshire.

When we say something is very **intriguing** we are using a word which comes directly from the French. It originally meant anything closely wrapped up or folded. It is connected with the word **intricate**. If you find anything so interesting that you become closely wrapped up in it you become **intrigued** by it.

Barrique in French means a large cask or barrel. In riots in the streets of French towns these large barrels were used to form defensive obstructions which become known as **barricades**, a word we adopted and use to this day.

Nephew, **niece** and **aunt** all came into our language from the French. If you turn to your English–French dictionary you will find that the modern French word for aunt is *tante*; but it should really be, and used originally to be, *ante* which gave us our word. In French nurseries the affectionate childish form ante-tante was used and it is from this that the modern French word comes. It is amusing to note that whereas we call a pawnbroker 'uncle', the French slang for the same sort of shop is 'aunt'.

Droit is the French for straight or direct. The person who could do anything in the most direct straightforward manner was called **adroit** which is exactly the English word we use today.

Brown is got by mixing red, yellow and black. The French word for it is *brun*, the feminine diminutive of this is **brunette (brunet)**, a word which we have taken straight into English as the opposite of **blonde (blond)**, which incidentally originally meant yellow and now means light or fair.

Look up the modern French word for a field; you will find it is *champ*. The older French word for a number of fields, or the countryside, was *campagne*. The military operations fought over such a stretch of countryside became a **campaign** which is how we get our English word for the same thing.

You probably know already that the French word for brother is *frère* and it is from this that our word **friar** comes,

meaning one of a brotherhood of men. It is the business of some friars to **preach**, and this word too comes from the French *precher*.

By the way, take a look at that word Canterbury. The pilgrims used to travel to the shrine of St. Thomas à Becket in Canterbury Cathedral on horseback at an easy pace somewhere between a trot and a gallop; it became known as a canterbury pace, or a **canter**.

French used to be the official Court language in England as we have seen and even today there survive a few ancient traces of this. When the Queen gives her consent to a Bill she says

'Le roy le veult', old fashioned French for the king wishes it. Take a look at the royal coat of arms and you will see the motto is in French 'Dieu et mon droit'. We have met this word 'droit' already in a slightly different sense. Here it means 'right'—so what does the whole motto mean?

The Order of the Garter has for its motto, 'Honi soit qui mal y pense', people very often translate this as 'evil be to him who evil thinks'. But this is wrong. Get out your French dictionary and work out the right translation.

 # Arabic

The Arabic language supplies us with a surprising number of words, some of which go back to the time of the Crusades. The first crusade was in 1096, the eighth and last in 1270; by the way the word **crusade** comes by a roundabout way from the Latin *cruciata*, meaning having the shape of a cross, because the Crusaders who were fighting to recover the Holy Lands from the Turks and Arabs marched into battle under the sign of the Cross.

The Arab definite article, which is equivalent to our word 'the', was *al*, which can be readily seen in **alchemist**, **algebra** and **alcohol**, all words taken from the Arabic. **Orange** is an interesting word; it comes from the Arabic *naranj* because the first oranges known in England came from that part of the world. Originally, therefore, people spoke about a norange but you can understand how easily this got corrupted into an orange.

There are several other words like this. What we now call an **adder**, for instance is really *a nadder*. In the West of England there is a Nadder valley and a river Nadder. Turn to the section about Saxon words and see what it says about nicknames.

The Arabs knew a good deal about astronomy when the rest of the world knew very little, and several of our astronomical terms come from them, particularly **nadir** and **zenith**. By zenith the Arabs meant the point in the heavens directly overhead, and the word has now come to mean the highest point reached by anything; nadir is the opposite of this, the lowest point.

Alcove is another word incorporating the Arab **al**. The cove part comes from an Arabic word *gobbah* which means a vault or small chamber.

When you ask somebody to pass the **sugar** you are using an almost pure Arabic word *sukkar*; a word with a similar meaning **syrup** also comes from the Arabic, so does **sherbet**, from the Arabic *shariba* meaning to drink.

Artichoke is an Arabic word, and don't forget there are two kinds of artichoke—the ordinary one of which you eat the fleshy bits of the leaves and the so-called Jerusalem artichoke of which you eat the roots.

Assassin is a very interesting word of Arabic descent. Now it means a person who is hired to kill somebody, or a murderer who kills a public personage. We speak about the assassination of a king or president, for instance. Originally in Arabic the word was *hashshashin* which meant people who took the drug called hashish be-

cause in the time of the Crusades certain Moslem fanatics who took this drug used to murder their political enemies in secret.

Admiral is a word with such strong English connections that it is a little surprising to realize that it comes from the Arabic and is really another form of *Emir* meaning a leader or prince. *Amir-al-bahr* was the Arabic phrase for the leader at sea and we eventually took the word over as admiral.

If you play chess you will know the term **checkmate** which means that you have managed to get your pieces in such a position that your opponent is unable to move his king anywhere and so you have won the game. Checkmate is simply our way of pronouncing the two Arabic words *shah*, a ruler or king, as, for instance, the Shah of Persia, and *mat* meaning dead.

⑨ Shakespeare

Nobody enjoyed words more than William Shakespeare. He lived in the time of Queen Elizabeth the First when English adventurers, like Sir Walter Raleigh, were sailing in their small ships all over the world and coming back with all sorts of new and exciting words.

Here is a list of some of the words introduced into English by Shake-speare. After each one you will see the name of the play in which it occurs; turn to the play in each case and see if you can find the word.

Alligator
This comes from the Spanish *el lagarto* meaning the lizard, and you can find it in Act V of Romeo and Juliet.

The earliest form of our word **hurri-cane**, which comes from the Spanish *huracan*, was the more exciting sounding *hurricano*. Shakespeare seized on this fine sounding word and used it in Troilus and Cressida in the line

"the dreadful spout
which shipmen do the
Hurricano call'.

If a person is looked up to by everybody we sometimes call him a **paragon**. The word comes from the Italian and Shakespeare was one of the first English writers to use it. Turn to the second act of Hamlet and you will find it spoken there by Hamlet himself.

Sonnet

in Italian simply meant a little sound; it is the diminutive form of *suono*. In English it is used to describe a poem of exactly fourteen lines, which have to rhyme according to a certain pattern. The word came into our language in Shakespeare's time and he uses it in the first act of the Merry Wives of Windsor.

As well as using individual words for the first time Shakespeare invented a whole series of phrases which we use time and time again in daily speech. Here is a list of a few of these phrases. Write them down and opposite each one your explanation of what it means and then see if you can find it in Shakespeare's plays.

to screw one's courage to the sticking-point (Macbeth)
to eat out of house and home (Henry IV Part 2)
to be hoist with one's own petard (Hamlet)
every inch a king (Lear)
more sinned against than sinning (Lear)
to the top of one's bent (Hamlet)

You will find in some cases that in long usage the phrases have become very slightly changed from the original form in Shakespeare.

Cannibal

Get out your atlas and find the Caribbean Islands. The tribes who inhabited them in Shakespeare's time were called by the Spanish *caribes* (see the picture opposite) and it is from this name that the word cannibal comes. Shakespeare introduced the word into English in the first act of Othello; see if you can spot exactly where.

10 Picturesque

Some words are like pictures, which is exactly what picturesque means, it comes from the Italian—*pittoresco*, in the style of a painter; they are like pictures because when you examine them they suddenly and often unexpectedly conjure up a vivid image in your mind. We have crammed a number of them into this little story. See how many you can find and then go on to see if your picture is accurate.

Alone, and dressed like a scarecrow, the thief left the back exit of the skyscraper. Looking crestfallen and showing signs of the white feather the blackguard climbed into his dilapidated car and sped across the city. He had hoped that everything would pan out all right but the police were after the culprit making every effort to check-

mate him. Soon he was caught. The time had come for him to eat humble-pie and atone for his sins; especially when the loot turned out to be a few tawdry beads. Two years seemed to be a trivial time to reform this eavesdropper.

Skyscraper

A vivid piece of word-making if there ever was one—a building so high that it scrapes against the sky! Some two hundred years before the Americans coined the word 'skyscraper', Shakespeare, when he wanted to give an idea of how high a hill was, had written 'the heaven-kissing hill'.

Alone

When you are alone you are all by yourself; there is only one of you; you are *all one*.

Atone

In exactly the same way when you atone for some fault you heal the breach that existed between you and somebody else, you are both *at one* again.

Blackguard

In medieval days when a king or great noble moved about the countryside he took everything he needed for living with him; thus one part of his wagon train consisted of the necessary cooking pots and pans, to say nothing of coal and other domestic requirements. The knights who rode in front as a protection were called the 'body guard', as they are today; when the Queen rides to open Parliament she is accompanied by a 'Queen's Body Guard' of mounted men. The servants who travelled in the rear with all the food and kitchen supplies were humorously referred to as *'the black guard.'*

Eavesdrop
Is to listen in to somebody else's secrets; it describes a person standing with his ear pressed against the wall of a house—so close that he was where the water from the eaves would drop on him. So someone trying to overhear a private conversation.

This would make a good start for an exciting story. Try to find out what the houses were like in Europe in the Middle Ages.

Dilapidated
Means tumbled down, in a bad state of repair, and it has that meaning because of the two Latin words from which it is made up: *di* meaning apart and *lapis* meaning a stone. So a dilapidated building is one whose stones have begun to fall down. By the way, if lapis means a stone what do you think the word lapidary means? Look it up in your dictionary and see if you were right.

Tawdry
A picturesque word indeed, because it really should be, of all things, Saint Audry! In the cathedral town of Ely there used to be a famous fair held every year on St. Audrey's feast day (October 17th). One of the features of the fair was a row of cheap jewellery booths at which necklaces were sold known as 'St. Audrey necklaces' and the word eventually became contracted into its present form.

Humble-pie
There is a catch in this one. It has nothing to do with humble. When a deer was hunted and killed the lords and ladies ate the flesh, or venison and the servants and followers made a pie out of the entrails, and the Saxon word for the entrails of deer was *umbles*.

To pan out
'I hope everything will pan out all right for you' we might say to a friend, without realising that we are really talking about the men who went prospecting and swirled the river water and mud about in a shallow pan to see if they could see a gleam of gold in it.

Culprit
For a good 'picturesque' word let us look at culprit. In days when a sort of Anglo-French was the official language of the Law Courts the prosecuting counsel would open his case for the crown with the formula *'Culpable; prest'* which meant 'the prisoner is guilty and I am ready to prove it'. The court proceedings were taken down in longhand and were always abbreviated where possible so in the written account what the prosecuting counsel said was put down as *'cul-prest'* which in time became corrupted to 'culprit', meaning guilty person.

Scarecrow
A common enough word but when you use it remember that it means exactly what it says—something put there to scare the crows away. In some country parts a scarecrow has the delightful name of 'boggart'.

Try to write a story of your own concerning a scarecrow. You may like to take the part of the scarecrow yourself or simply to include it in a picturesque story of the countryside.

Crestfallen
In cock-fighting the bird which was getting the worst of it began to droop its crest.

White feather

Is another word from cock-fighting; to 'show the white feather' means to show signs of cowardice because a white feather in the tail of a game cock was considered to be a sign of a bird without much courage.

Some of the words we use most constantly are those connected with time. **Day** comes from an Anglo-Saxon word *daeg* and is the time in which the earth makes one complete revolution on its axis.

Each day is divided into twenty-four **hours**, from the Latin word *hora*, and *we* now reckon our airline timetables according to the twenty-four hour clock system. Each of these hours is divided into sixty **minutes**, from the Latin *minuta* meaning small: each of these minutes is again divided into sixty parts and because this is the second division these small units of time are called **seconds**.

The days of the week take their names from Anglo-Saxon. **Sunday** is sunnan daeg, the day specifically set aside for the worship of the *sun*, just as **Monday** was dedicated to the *moon*. The Romans called the goddess of the moon Diana and built temples for her.

Tiw, the Anglo-Saxon god of war gives his name to **Tuesday** and it is curious that the French for Tuesday should be Mardi which comes from Mars who was also a god of war.

Odin or *Woden* the god of storms, the greatest of the Teutonic deities, gives his name to **Wednesday**. Odin lived in Valhalla, the home of the gods, and when he wanted news of the world he sent as messengers two ravens who otherwise sat perched on his shoulder.

Thursday comes from *Thor* the god of thunder and **Friday** from the goddess *Freya*, wife of the mighty Odin and goddess of marriage. With **Saturday** we come to *Saturn* the deity of agriculture and harvest.

Month comes from the Anglo-Saxon word for the moon, *mona*, because once every month the moon makes a complete circuit round the earth. There are twelve months in a year and their names are interesting. **January** is named after the Roman god *Janus* who was supposed to be the keeper of the gates of heaven. As January is the first month Janus was represented as standing at the entrance or doorway of the year. He is always represented as having two faces, one looking forward into the future and one looking back on the past. His temple in Rome was kept open during time of war, and closed during peace. It was nearly always open.

The original Roman year had only ten months in it. Julius Caesar shortened the months and added two more— January and February. The name **February** comes from the Latin word *februa* which means a cleaning or cleansing because a religious festival of purification was held on the fifteenth day of the month.

March, which until 1752 was reckoned as the first month of the legal year, is called after the Roman god of war *Mars*, after whom the planet Mars is also named.

In **April** trees and plants, and indeed all living things, begin to open to the sun and the Latin word meaning to open, *aperire*, has given us the name of this which is one of the loveliest of all the months.

Maia was the Roman goddess of growth and increase, so it is natural

TIW· ·WODENS·

THOR FREYA SATURN

that the month **May** in which everything begins to swell and grow should be called May.

June is probably named after *Juno* the beautiful but jealous wife of Jupiter and Queen of the heavens who drove about in a chariot drawn by strutting peacocks.

July used to be called Quintilis, meaning the fifth month which it was in the original Roman calendar. It was renamed July in honour of *Julius* Caesar who was born in it.

In the same way **August** was so called after *Augustus* Caesar, the wise and good ruler who succeeded Julius Caesar and who was emperor of Rome at the time Jesus Christ was born.

The last four months of the year, **September, October, November** and **December** remind us of something already noted, that originally the year consisted of ten months: *Septem* means seven, *octo* eight, *novem* nine and *decem* ten, which explains these names.

Space

The world on which we live is a tiny speck floating in what we call **space**. Space is **infinite**, which means without end, and comes from the two Latin words *in*, not and *finis*, an end. In that infinite space we can see the sun, which as we know gives us the word **Sunday**; the moon, from which we get **Monday**; the planets and the stars.

The name **planet** comes from a Greek word *planasthai* meaning to wander about, and the planets are so called because they travel in orbits round the sun and are not fixed in position like the stars.

In order of distance from the sun the planets are Mercury, Venus, the Earth, Mars, Jupiter, Saturn, Uranus, Neptune and Pluto. Planets were thought to have an influence on human beings according to the date on which a man was born, and at least two words still give evidence of this; we speak of a man being **mercurial** in temperament if he is quick and lively and liable to sudden changes of mood; and we say a man is **saturnine** if he is inclined to be heavy and dull.

Many people still living can remember the time when no such thing as an plane existed. There used to be a popular saying 'Oh, that will happen when pigs can fly' which you used if you wanted to say that you thought something would never take place; and when Lord Brabazon, who was the first qualified pilot and the very first Englishman to fly, went on his first flight he actually took up with him a small pig just to prove how out of date the old saying had become!

Now men are actually travelling to the moon and exploring the vastness of space. This means that a whole series of fresh words are coming into daily use; and it would be interesting to look at a few of them.

Rocket—this is particularly interesting because, although the rocket journeying into space is a very new thing, the word itself is old. When weaving was done in practically every home in the land the **distaff** was a very common household object. A distaff was a cleft stick about three feet long on which the wool used in weaving was wound. The old English name for a distaff was a *rock*. When a firework was made with a long stick attached to it for shooting up into the air it looked very much like a small distaff, or diminutive rock, and somebody dubbed it rocket. So the newest, most complicated piece of machinery is connected in its name with one of the oldest and simplest of crafts.

Capsule is another word we came across in space travel; this comes from the Latin *capsa* meaning a box, of which there was a diminutive form *capsula* used to describe a little container of any sort. The capsule of a space vehicle is the small compartment at the top of it usually packed with scientific instruments.

A **satellite** simply means some small thing which moves round a bigger one and the word comes direct from the Latin *satelles* which was used originally to describe an attendant, or personal body guard, who was always moving close to the person who employed him.

Satellites go in **orbit** around other bodies and for the origin of the word orbit we must go again to the Latin when we find the word *orbis* meaning first of all a ring or circle, and then any circular, or roughly circular, thing such as the track that a satellite takes in the sky.

Cosmonaut, **astronaut** and **lunarnaut** are all words in common use now. The first thing that strikes us about them is that they all end in the same syllable— naut. What does this naut business mean? Once again a very modern thing is linked with an old one. The Greek word for a ship is *naus*, and the legendary heroes who sailed with Jason in the ship Argo to find the Golden Fleece were called the Argonauts.

So *naut* means a brave explorer of any kind and in this, the space age, we have made use of it in the three words cosmonaut, astronaut, and lunarnaut. You probably realize what astronaut and lunarnaut mean, but cosmonaut is worth looking at.

The Greek philosophers considered that in the very beginning of things the world was in utter disorder and confusion which they called **chaos**. We still use the word a lot; if we want to describe something, for instance, which isn't properly organized or thought out we say it was 'absolutely chaotic'. When this original state of confusion was shaped into an ordered and balanced creation the Greeks called it the cosmos, by which they meant not only the whole world but the whole universe.

So our cosmonaut is an explorer of the universe and two old words have come together to describe a very modern thing.

Proper Names

Wellington
Commanded the British Army at the Battle of Waterloo in 1815 and was known as the 'Iron Duke'. He gave his name to rubber knee boots which in England are called **wellingtons**.

Cardigan
Led the famous, but useless, charge which was made by the Light Brigade at Balaclava in the Crimean War. Very fashion conscious and the knitted woollen jacket we wear is called after him.

Raglan
Lord Raglan lost his right arm at the Battle of Waterloo. He wore an overcoat, with the sleeve in one piece with the shoulder, which has been named after him.

Sandwich
A notorious gambler. He spent many hours at the gaming tables and became so involved that he would not leave for meals so had cold meat between bread brought to him at the tables.

As with these things named after English aristocrats, many names have come to be used to describe an object or action associated with a person or place.

ampère	*A. M. Ampère*, French physicist.
bayonet	*Bayonne*, France. The town where it was first made.
bobby	*Sir Robert Peel* founded the police force in 1829.
bohemian	*Bohemia*, Eastern Europe. Home of the gypsies.
boycott	*Capt. Boycott*, Irish Land Agent.
bunsen	*R. W. Bunsen*, chemist and inventor.
cardigan	*Earl of Cardigan*. Crimea War 1855.
cereal	*Ceres*, Roman goddess of grain and harvest.
diesel	*Rudolf Diesel*, German. Worked at Krupp Factory.
echo	Nymph *Echo* in Greek mythology.
fez	*Fez*, a town in Morocco.
guillotine	French physician *J. I. Guillotin* in 1789.
hamburger	*Hamburg*, Germany.

THE DUKE OF WELLINGTON

LORD RAGLAN

EARL OF CARDIGAN

THE EARL OF SANDWICH

mackintosh	*Charles Mackintosh* (1766–1843), invented the material.	sandwich	John Montagu, *Earl of Sandwich* 1718–92.
melba	Australian opera singer from Melbourne.	volcano	*Vulcan*, blacksmith of the Roman Gods.
morse-code	*S. F. B. Morse*, American, invented a dots and dashes alphabet 1872.	*volt*	*Alessandro Volta* 19th Cent. Italian physicist.
		watt	*James Watt*, 19th Cent. Scottish inventor.
panama	Central American country.	wellington	Arthur, 1st *Duke of Wellington* 1769–1852.
raglan	*Lord Raglan*, Crimea War.		

Sir Miles of Twyne

33

14 Occupational Names

A person's real name is his first one, what we call his Christian name because it is given him in the Christian sacrament of baptism, as John, Henry, George, and so on; but in a village there might be several Johns, and so to make clear which one you were talking about it became usual to refer to John Baker or John Smith or John Thatcher, according to what occupation the particular person followed. These we call *surnames*.

The three names already quoted are obvious examples of names taken from what a man did—by the way, **Baxter** was originally a woman baker, and in a similar way **Weaver** was clearly a man who wove cloth and a woman who did the same job was a **Webster**—both of which are of course established surnames.

A **wright** was a man who wrought, i.e. worked and made things in wood, so you may perhaps know a Mr. **Cartwright** or a Mr. **Wheelwright** or a Mr. **Sievewright** among your friends.

The man who looked after animals was referred to as a *herd* so in time the names **Shepherd** and **Coward**, meaning cowherd, came into being. The word **Howard** is of the same class and is really a corruption of hogherd; a similar sort of mispronunciation has given us **Goddard** which originally was the name borne by the man who looked after the goats, or the goatherd.

Mason, **Thatcher** and **Tyler** are all straightforward occupational names. One of the most important buildings in the countryside used to be the mill and it is not surprising that **Miller** is a fairly common name—nearly all millers are nicknamed 'dusty'; can you think why?

A name which is not so obvious is **Palmer**. This was given to a man who had been on pilgrimage to the Holy Land and, as a proof that he *had* been there, brought back a leaf of palm.

Another surname which might puzzle you at first is **Lorrimer** which, believe it or not, means a man who makes bits for horses' bridles. It comes from the French word lorian meaning a thong of leather from which the bridles, and originally the bits themselves, were made.

Latimer is also a little puzzling, largely because it is a mis-spelling. It should be *latiner* meaning the learned person who, when very few people could read or write, was capable of writing things down in what was then the common language of books, Latin.

If a mill was an important feature of village life so were the wells which were the main source of water supply, so a man who knew how to construct a well soon got the surname of **Weller**.

An old word for a fox was a *tod*. This has now gone out of use in that sense but **Todhunter**, the man who hunted foxes, is still a fairly common surname.

Spencer, too, is a name frequently seen. In big houses the buttery, or place from which various stores were *dispensed*, was called the **spence**. The man in charge of giving out the goods was called the *dispenser*, shortened to **Spenser**.

Every village used to have its pound in which straying animals were *im-*

pounded, the man whose duty it was to look after the pound naturally enough got the name **Pounder**.

Smith was the man who smote, and fashioned, things in metal. One particular kind of smith whose occupation has become a surname was the **arrow-smith**. There is another surname looking entirely different yet meaning precisely the same thing; this is **Fletcher**, from the French word *flèche*.

In the same way the man who looked after the game in a park or game preserve was called *Warrener* sometimes shortened to **Warner**. Try to find out the origin of your own surname and those of other people you know.

15 Means of Transport

Many forms of transport have fascinating beginnings and interesting names. **Balloons** and ballooning were once very popular, especially in the nineteenth century. The word comes to us from the Italian *ballone*—a large ball. Hot air and later hydrogen were used to inflate spheres made from paper and linen which carried a basket suspended underneath. It was in the balloon that man first enjoyed suspension in the air and travel across the sky. Later the **glider** added to this experience. The glider which we now know as an engineless aeroplane takes us back to the days when brave and adventurous men strapped wings to themselves and attempted to glide from high places like the birds they had observed sweeping down with rigid wings using the air currents to keep them from losing height. It was not until the nineteenth century that Sir George Caley built and flew the first full-sized glider.

Moving without the aid of engines brings us to that amazing vehicle the **bicycle**. *Bi* meaning two and cycle from the Greek *cyclon* meaning wheel give us a word for a two-wheeled vehicle. Likewise **unicycle** and **tricycle**, uni meaning one and tri three. Make a list of other words which use the prefixes uni, bi and tri, and check them with your dictionary.

There are several types of bicycles which have picturesque names. The **hobby-horse** was a wooden backbone with two wheels, the rear one fixed and the front one fitted to a pivoted fork. Ridden astride, pushing off with his feet, the action reminded people of the hobby-horse which had been a toy since medieval days. It was sometimes called a **dandy-horse**.

The **bone-shaker** was simply a bicycle without rubber tyres which shook your bones as you rode over the rough or cobbled streets. The **penny farthing** was so called because it had one large wheel and one small one like an English penny and a farthing.

The Latin word *carrus*—a four-wheeled vehicle—gave the Romans their carriage with back seat only a **chariot** and from *char* we get **car**; put a motor in your car and we have **motor-car**. In the United States this is often called an automobile, which literally means something which moves by itself.

In the fourteenth century there was a clumsy long carriage called a *char* for carrying the Court followers and their baggage. This gave way in later days to the **char-a-banc** or touring coach, a long vehicle, with many forward-facing seats for scenic holiday excursions. *Char-a-bancs* is the French for benched carriage.

The days of Queen Victoria added many names of vehicles to our language, particularly in connection with horse-drawn transport. She even gave her name to one such coach—the **Victoria**, which was a low, elegant carriage, from which the upper classes could see and be seen when driving out. **Coaches** had spread through Europe in the sixteenth century, the word for them in English goes back to *kocsi*, a word of Hungarian origin.

The French word *haquenée* means a common horse for ordinary riding, usually of poor quality and so a carriage drawn by such horses became known as a **Hackney-coach**. These could be hired for short journeys in towns like the present day taxi. The Hackney-coach, one specifically for hire, was used in London until the '**cab**, from the French *cabriolet*, which was introduced from Paris in 1820 and which in turn gave way to the taximeter cab or **taxi** as the motor-car developed.

Omnibus, now usually shortened to **bus**, derives from the Latin *omnibus*— for all, and so a form of transport available to everybody. The first buses were horse drawn.

Moving to the sea or rather below it **submarine** needs little explanation; *sub* —under, *mare*—sea. **Cruiser** and **yacht** are mentioned in the chapter about words of Dutch origin. It has always been the right of races or people who invented things to name them and there are many English words like **railway** and **jet** which you can add to your lists without any help.

But we must end with the latest addition to our many forms of earth transport. **Hovercraft** does exactly what it says—hovers above the land or sea. This amazing machine was a British invention and has even shot the rapids of the Orinoco River in South America. In the United States this is known as an Air-cushioned-Vehicle, contracted to A.C.V.

You may like to invent a transporter of the future and a name for it.

16 America India S. Africa & Australia

There was a time, not very long ago, when if you looked at a map of the world you would have seen India, Australia, New Zealand, Canada and South Africa, and many other places besides, were British Colonies.

British soldiers and sailors went to these places, traders went there and civil servants and settlers: and from all these far-off lands a stream of new words came into the English language to enrich it. Very often the words came to England in a corrupt form but they are still vivid and useful additions to the vocabulary.

From the long association with India we get a number of words. There was a Hindu word *thag* meaning a member of a band of robbers and murderers who used to strangle their victims. We changed this into **thug** and still use it in much the same sense. **Char** meaning tea, 'a cup of char', is another word which comes direct to Britain from Hindustani.

The Urdu word for dust is *khak*. From this we get the name **khaki** given to the dust coloured uniforms first worn by British troops about 1860.

The Boer War, which was fought in South Africa from 1899–1902 brought a whole crop of fresh words.

Commando dates from that time; so does **kraal**, which originally meant a fenced enclosure for cattle and later came to be applied to any enclosure with a fence round it.

In South Africa at that time oxen were very largely used for drawing the wagons and from this we get the two words **in-span**, to put the animals in their place in the team at the beginning of the day, and **outspan**, to take them out again at the end of the journey. **Span** comes from the Dutch word *spannen* meaning to fasten.

Once the oxen were inspanned they would set off on the day's **trek** which is another word that came to us from South Africa where *trekken* means to pull or draw. A trek was the distance between one stopping place and another, which in coaching days in England used to be called a **stage**. At the end of the day's trek the oxen would be outspanned and the wagons formed into a protective circle around the place of encampment. This circle of wagons was called a **laager**, another South African word. This laager, or encampment, would probably be made on the **veldt** which in South Africa means the open countryside and is in fact connected with our own word *field* since both words go back originally to the German *feld*.

Australia has added a number of words to current English. Australia is a country of immense distances and of vast open spaces and one of the most expressive words we have borrowed from the Australians is **outback** to describe the country and the lonely settlements tucked far away from the normal regions of living. **Back of beyond** is another picturesque phrase meaning the same thing.

The Australian word for a newcomer

from the Old Country is **pommy**, and it is an odd thing that nobody really knows what the origin of this word is. It has been suggested that the red and white of the Englishman's cheeks, reminiscent of the colouring of a pomegranate, gave rise to the word, but this may not be true.

In the outback the **bushman** is a great figure, and this word *bush* is worth looking at. Its origin goes right back to Roman days and the Latin word *bosco* which meant a wood; so **boscobel**, when King Charles hid for safety in an oak tree while the Roundhead soldiers of Cromwell were searching for him, means simply **bosco bello**, that is, the lovely wood. This incident was just after the English Civil Wars.

The bushman's tea pot is called a **billy** or **billycan** which is a word coined by Australians, and the natives who were living in the bush long before the white man ever went there are called the **Aborigines** because they were there from the beginning, Latin *ab*=from and orgine=beginning.

Where the English use the word farm the Australians generally speak of a **station** and a farm hand at a station is called a **jackaroo** which is a combination of Jack and Kangaroo. You can see this name **Jack** being used in all sorts of combinations: jacktar for a sailor; cheapjack for a man who goes from door to door selling things; a steeplejack and a jack-of-all-trades are examples.

The word **kangaroo** itself comes, of course, from Australia; so does **wallaby** which is merely a smaller version of the same animal.

Dingo is the aboriginal name for the wild, or half-wild, dog to be found in the bush. By a similarity of sound the word reminds us of **jingo** and **jingoism** which means excessive and aggressive nationalism; it came to have this meaning in a curious manner. In 1875 the Russians were threatening to take Constantinople from the Turks; England didn't want this to happen and a good deal of public feeling on the matter was whipped up. Part of this campaign was a music-hall song which became immensely popular, the chorus of which ran:

'We don't want to fight
But by jingo, if we do
We've got the men, we've got the ships
And we've got the money too.'

and it was from this popular song that **jingoism** got its present meaning.

The language which was taken to Massachusetts by the Pilgrim Fathers in 1620 was, of course, English as it was spoken at that time—Elizabethan English. You can see a picture opposite of the first landing at Massachusetts Bay.

Since that date, and especially in the last 150 years, America has taken in literally millions of immigrants—Irish, Italians, Poles, Germans and Scandinavians amongst them. This hodgepodge—or hotch-potch—of different people has given an enormous liveliness to the sort of English that is spoken in America, and a whole lot of vivid words and phrases have come back to England from the U.S.A.

Where the English talk about a pavement the Americans say **sidewalk**; the English speak of a chemist's shop, the Americans call it a **drugstore**. The English go up in a lift, the Americans use an **elevator**; at the garage an Englishman asks for petrol, the American calls for **gas**—hence we get the expression to step on the gas, meaning to get a move on. **Commuter**, meaning a person travelling for the same short run on the railway everyday, is now in use in England too. **Blizzard, bogus,** and **rowdy** all came from America and have now been adopted in England. **Co-ed**, short for co-educational is another example of an American invention and so is the useful word **streamline** which originally referred to the design of planes and now means to make anything more simple and easily worked. A **hand-out** was originally a free meal handed out to a **hobo**, or as the English would say, tramp. **Getaway** and **hideout** are two more Americanisms. **Dope, pep, bootlegger, stunt, lynch** and **highbrow** have all become part of the vocabulary.

Language is constantly being enriched from such contacts and by the necessity of finding new words to describe new discoveries; but a good deal of old-established slang is still in use and we might end up by reminding ourselves of one of the most amusing classes of it—the rhyming slang which the quick wit of the London cockney brought to perfection: 'Cain and Abel' for table; 'mince pies' for eyes; 'plates of meat' for feet are three well known examples. A wife was referred to as the 'trouble and strife' and a flight of stairs as the 'apples and pears'.

Sometimes the rhyming word is left out, thus: 'he was so elephants he couldn't get up the apples' means 'he was so drunk (elephant's trunk) and he couldn't get up the stairs (apples and pears).

But whether you are writing good English in an essay or talking colloquially in daily conversation you are using *words*, and as we have tried to show you in this short book words are interesting things often with fascinating and complicated histories behind them.

17 Word Making

You can have lots of fun making up words for yourself. Every generation of youngsters does it.

Super-duper is a good modern example; and I remember a young girl of about eight years old describing a heap of dishevelled bed-clothes as being 'all **hofty-wofty**'.

By the way, you should look up the word **dishevelled** in your dictionary and see exactly what it means and how it came to mean it.

I once heard a boy say 'I feel very spirity today' which I thought was a splendid way of saying that he was full of life; when I took the same boy to look at an old tumbled-down mill he was rather disappointed and said, after a pause, 'The mill doesn't look very milly to me'. Writing which was full of blots and messes was described by one bright schoolboy as **glotty** and someone who simply couldn't be dragged away from the T.V. set was called a **vidiot**. Those who creep unwillingly to school are known as **linger-longers**.

Double sounding words like **shilly-shally** are fun to make up. Think of some of them:

> Ding-dong
> Sing-song
> Namby-pamby
> Wishy-washy
> Willy-nilly
> Zigzag
> Pitter-patter

You can probably think of half a dozen more to add to the list.

Anagram. This odd looking word is quite simple really; it comes directly from the Greek *ana* meaning again and *gramma* meaning a letter; different words made up of the same letters are called anagrams. An easy example is **live** and **evil**. A more complicated one is **stop** which can also be turned into **tops, pots, post** and **opts**.

One very clever anagram can be composed from the name of the famous admiral **Horatio Nelson**; the letters which make up his name can be turned into the Latin phrase **honor est a nilo** which, when you remember that one of Nelson's greatest victories was at the battle of the Nile, is very suitable. Can you discover some other anagrams?

Another strange looking word is **palindrome**. Once again this comes from the Greek and it means to *run back again*; it is used to describe a word which reads exactly the same forwards and backwards. A very simple example is **dad**; some five letter palindromes are **level, madam, rotor**.

Sometimes a whole sentence can be made into a palindrome. You probably know that Napoleon after being defeated and captured was imprisoned on the island of Elba, and some clever person, thinking of this fact, made up the following sentence: **'Able was I ere I saw Elba'**—spell it backwards and see what you get!

Can you think of any words which are the same forwards and backwards?

You can play an amusing game making **word ladders**. Here is an example:

Dog	Hat
Dot	Cat
Hot	

NELSON

NAPOLEON

You will see that starting with the word **dog** I have made a series of new words *changing only one letter each time* until finally the word **cat** is arrived at so that dog has become changed into cat.

Another example is **pen** which can be put into **pot** like this:

> **Pen**
> **Pet**
> **Pot**

Using this same method, can you change **cold** into **hate**?

There are so many words in the English language that it is possible to find exactly the right one to describe pretty well anything you can see, or any emotion you can feel; so when you are writing, or talking, don't always be content to use the same old words and phrases that everybody uses, but pause for a moment to see if you can't find some less usual, picturesque word which expresses exactly what you are trying to say.

aborigine	Australian	billycan	Australian
acrobat	Greek	biped	Roman
adder	Arabic	biscuit	Roman
admiral	Arabic	blackguard	Picturesque
adroit	French	blizzard	American
afternoon	Roman	blonde	French
against	Roman	bobby	Proper Names
agriculture	Roman	bodge	Dutch
alchemist	Arabic	bodger	Dutch
alcohol	Arabic	bogus	American
alcove	Arabic	bohemian	Proper Names
algebra	Arabic	bone-shaker	Transport
alligator	Shakespeare	boom	Dutch
alone	Picturesque	boor	South African
aloof	Dutch	bootlegger	American
alphabet	Greek	botch	Dutch
altar	Roman	bow	Saxon
altitude	Roman	boycott	Proper Names
ampere	Proper Names	brink	Danish
anagram	Fun with Words	brown	French
April	Time	brunette	French
Arrowsmith	Surnames	bunsen	Proper Names
artichoke	Arabic	burn	Saxon
assassin	Arabic	bus	Transport
astronaut	Space	bushman	Australian
athlete	Greek	-by	Danish
atone	Picturesque	cab	Transport
August	Time	cabin	French
aunt	French	cabinet	French
auspice	Roman	camp	Roman
autocracy	Greek	campaign	French
autocrat	Greek	candidate	Roman
avast	Dutch	cannibal	Shakespeare
aviary	Roman	canter	French
awkward	Danish	capsule	Space
back of beyond	Australian	car	Transport
balloon	Transport	cardigan	Proper Names
barricades	French	Cartwright	Surnames
Baxter	Surnames	castle	Norman
bayonet	Proper Names	cavalry	French
beam	Dutch	chancellor	Norman
beef	Saxon, Norman	chaos	Space
bicycle	Transport	char	Indian
bilateral	Roman	char-a-banc	Transport

chariot	Transport	dope	American
chase	French	drugstore	American
cheap	Saxon	easel	Danish
cheapjack	Saxon	eavesdrop	Picturesque
checkmate	Arabic	echo	Proper Names
chivalry	French	elevator	American
churlish	Saxon	falcon	French
cinema	Greek	fan	Roman
co-ed	American	fanatic	Roman
collision	Roman	February	Time
commando	South African	fez	Proper Names
commuter	American	field	Saxon
companion	Roman	Fletcher	Surnames
compassion	Roman	forenoon	Time
contend	Roman	friar	French
contradict	Roman	Friday	Time
cosmonaut	Space	gas	American
count	Norman	getaway	American
cover	French	glotty	Fun with Words
covert	French	glider	Transport
Coward	Surnames	goatherd	Saxon
crestfallen	Picturesque	Goddard	Surnames
crook	Danish	Guillotine	Proper Names
cruiser	Dutch	Hackney-coach	Transport
crusade	Arabic	hamburger	Proper Names
culprit	Picturesque	hand-out	American
cup	Roman	heliography	Greek
curfew	Norman	herd	Saxon
daisy	Saxon	herdsman	Saxon
dandelion	Norman	hideout	American
Dandy-horse	Transport	hobby-horse	Transport
darkness	Saxon	hobo	American
dawn	Saxon	hofty-wofty	Fun with Words
day	Saxon, Time	home	Saxon
December	Time	hour	Time
delirious	Roman	Hovercraft	Transport
democracy	Greek	Howard	Surnames
dew	Saxon	hoy	Dutch
diesel	Proper Names	huff	Dutch
dilapidated	Picturesque	humble-pie	Picturesque
ding-dong	Fun with Words	hurricane	Shakespeare
dingo	Australian	-hurst	Saxon
dishevelled	Fun with Words	husband	Danish
distaff	Space	infinite	Space

intricate	French	nephew	French
intrigued	French	niece	French
intriguing	French	night	Saxon
Jackaroo	Australian	noon	Roman
January	Time	November	Time
jet	Transport	October	Time
July	Time	orange	Arabic
June	Time	orbit	Space
kangaroo	Australian	outback	Australian
khaki	Indian	palindrome	Fun with Words
kraal	South African	Palmer	Surnames
laager	South African	Panama	Proper Names
landscape	Dutch	panic	Greek
Latimer	Surnames	pan-out	Picturesque
law	Danish	paragon	Shakespeare
-ley	Saxon	parliament	Norman
light	Saxon	parlour	Norman
linger-longer	Fun with Words	pedometer	Greek
Lorrimer	Surnames	pen	Roman
lunarnaut	Space	pence	Roman
lynch	American	penknife	Roman
Mackintosh	Proper Names	penny-farthing	Transport
March	Time	pep	American
Mason	Surnames	philately	Greek
master	Norman	philharmonic	Greek
May	Time	philosopher	Greek
melba	Proper Names	phone	Greek
mercurial	Space	phonetics	Greek
microbe	Greek	photograph	Greek
micrometer	Greek	pitter-patter	Fun with Words
microscope	Greek	planet	Space
mile	Roman	pommy	Australian
milestone	Roman	pork	Saxon,Norman
Miller	Surnames	port	Roman
minute	Time	post	Roman
Monday	Time	pound	Roman
-monger	Roman	Pounder	Surnames
month	Time	preach	French
moon	Space	rabbit	French
Morse-code	Proper Names	rabble	Dutch
mortgage	Norman	Raglan	Proper Names
mutton	Saxon	railway	Transport
nadir	Arabic	real	Norman
namby-pamby	Fun with Words	red	French

reindeer	Danish	telegram	Greek
reward	Norman	telegraph	Greek
riding	Danish	telephone	Greek
rocket	Space	telephoto	Greek
Sandwich	Proper Names	telescope	Greek
satellite	Space	television	Greek
Saturday	Time	Thatcher	Surnames
saturnine	Space	thrift	Danish
scales	Danish	thug	Indian
scarecrow	Picturesque	Thursday	Time
scoff	Dutch	Todhunter	Surnames
scold	Dutch	-ton	Saxon
score	Danish	town	Saxon
second	Time	trek	South African
September	Time	tricycle	Transport, Greek
Shepherd	Surnames	Tuesday	Time
shepherd	Saxon	Tyler	Surnames
sherbet	Arabic	unicycle	Transport
shilly-shally	Fun with Words	veal	Saxon
sidewalk	American	veldt	South African
Sievewright	Surnames	Victoria	Transport
sing-song	Fun with Words	vidiot	Fun with Words
skill	Danish	volcano	Proper Names
sky	Danish	volt	Proper Names
skyscraper	Picturesque	waggon	Dutch
Smith	Surnames	wain	Dutch
snare	Danish	wallaby	Australian
snub	Danish	waning	Saxon
sonnet	Shakespeare	Warner	Surnames
sovereign	Norman	warrant	Norman
span	South African	watt	Proper Names
speedometer	Greek	waxing	Saxon
Spence	Surnames	Weaver	Surnames
Spenser	Surnames	Webster	Surnames
streamline	American	Wednesday	Time
stunt	American	Weller	Surnames
submarine	Transport	Wellington	Proper Names
sugar	Arabic	Wheelwright	Surnames
sun	Space	white	Roman
Sunday	Time	white feather	Picturesque
syrup	Arabic	Whitsunday	Saxon
taxi	Transport	willy-nilly	Fun with Words
taximeter	Greek	wishy-washy	Fun with Words
tawdry	Picturesque	window	Danish